For Phyllis

The Brothers Grimm

Thorn Rose

Pictures By Errol Le Cain

Bradbury Press   Scarsdale, New York

Text and illustrations © Errol Le Cain 1975. All rights reserved. Library of Congress Catalog Card Number: 75-16835. Manufactured in the United States of America. First American edition published by Bradbury Press, Inc. 1977. ISBN: 0-87888-086-0

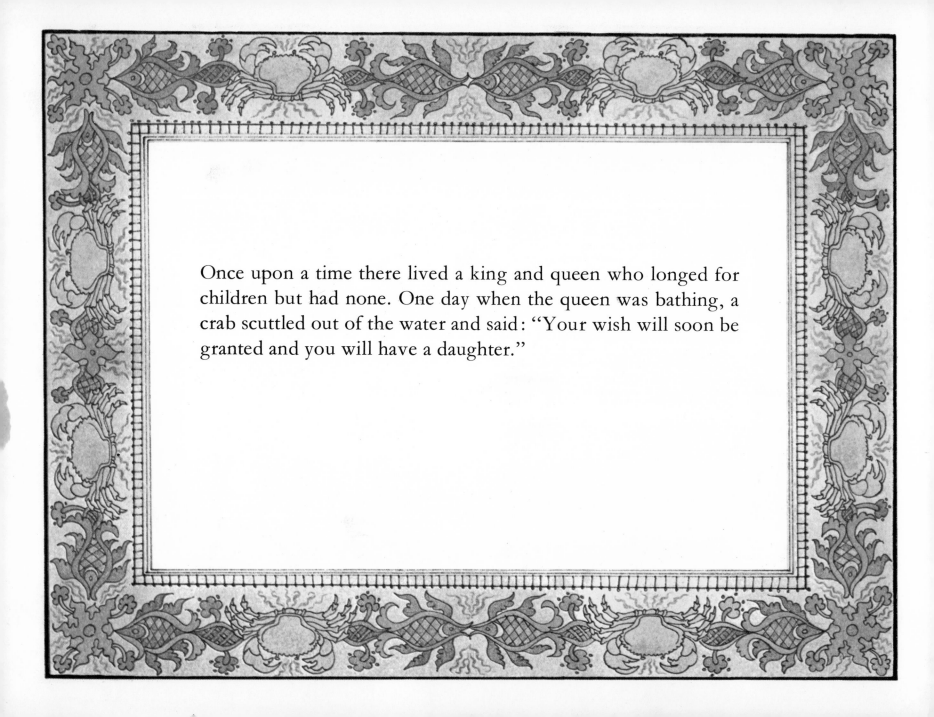

Once upon a time there lived a king and queen who longed for children but had none. One day when the queen was bathing, a crab scuttled out of the water and said: "Your wish will soon be granted and you will have a daughter."

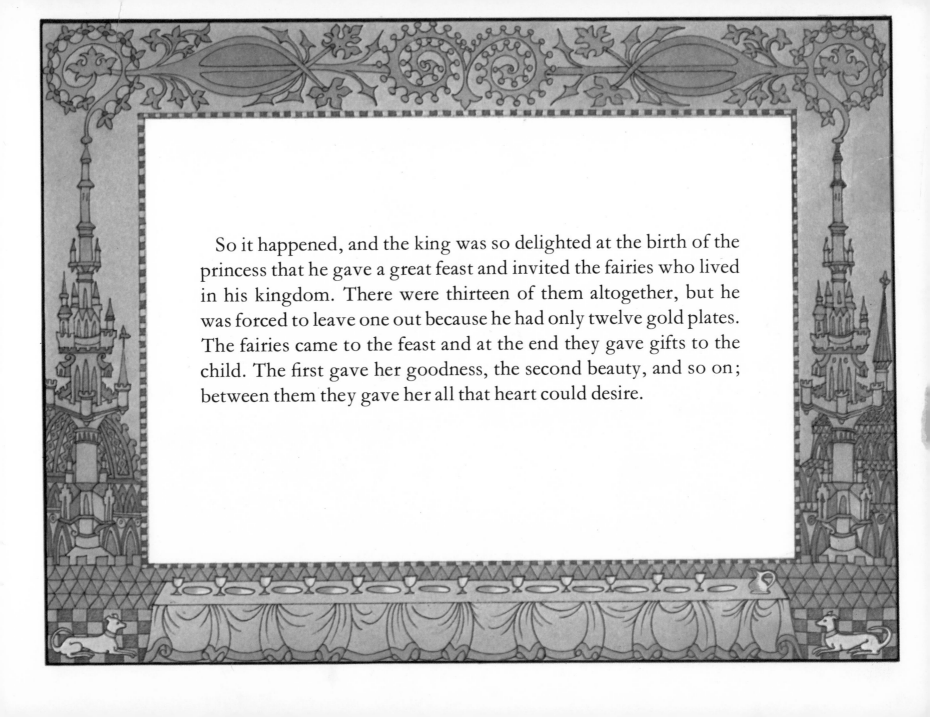

So it happened, and the king was so delighted at the birth of the princess that he gave a great feast and invited the fairies who lived in his kingdom. There were thirteen of them altogether, but he was forced to leave one out because he had only twelve gold plates. The fairies came to the feast and at the end they gave gifts to the child. The first gave her goodness, the second beauty, and so on; between them they gave her all that heart could desire.

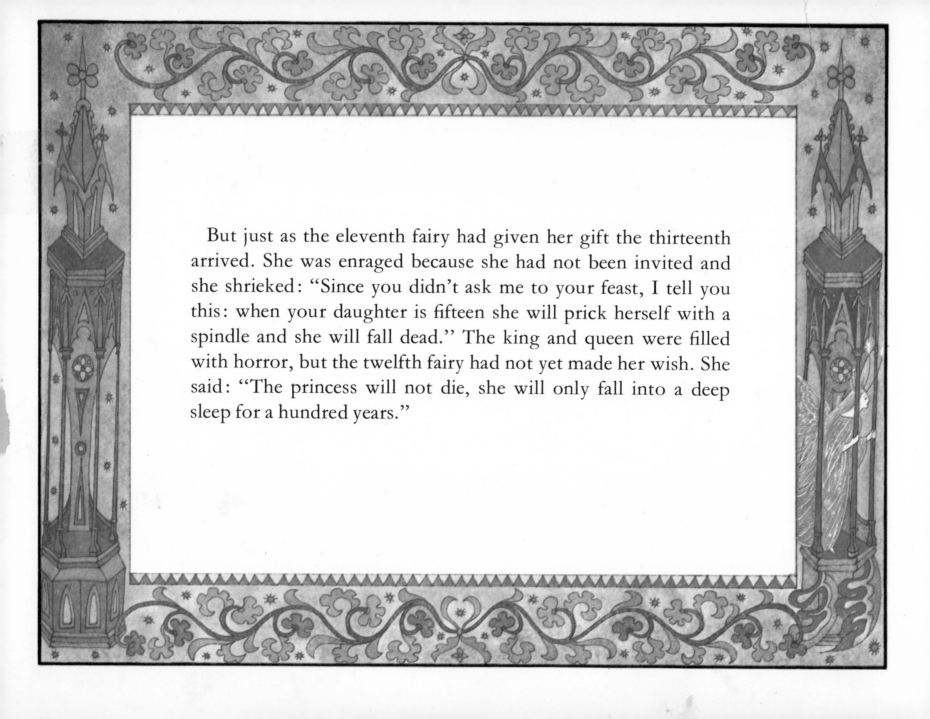

But just as the eleventh fairy had given her gift the thirteenth arrived. She was enraged because she had not been invited and she shrieked: "Since you didn't ask me to your feast, I tell you this: when your daughter is fifteen she will prick herself with a spindle and she will fall dead." The king and queen were filled with horror, but the twelfth fairy had not yet made her wish. She said: "The princess will not die, she will only fall into a deep sleep for a hundred years."

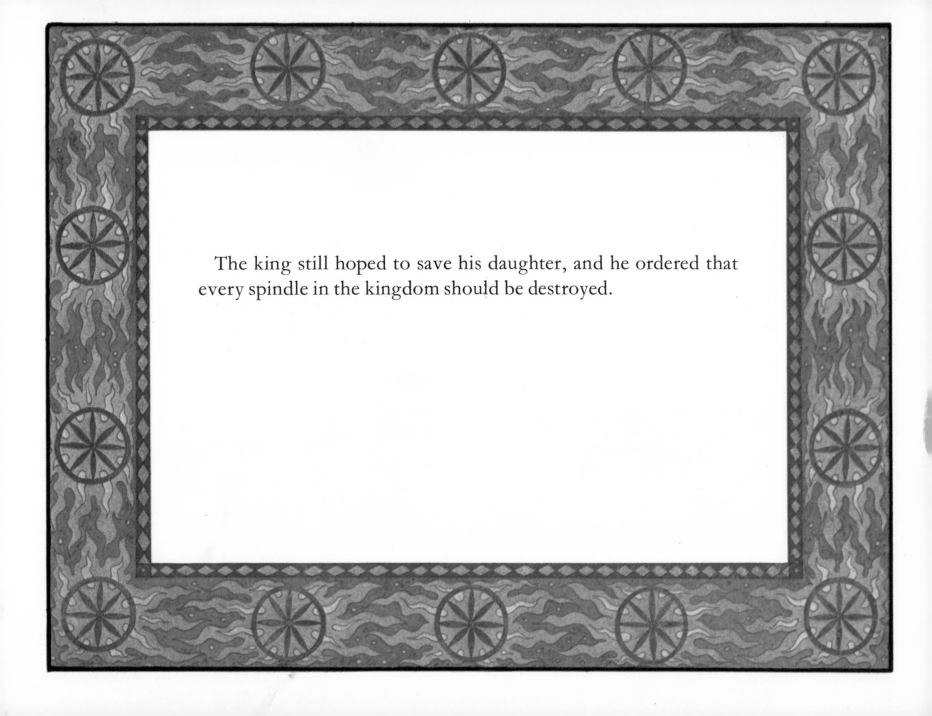

The king still hoped to save his daughter, and he ordered that every spindle in the kingdom should be destroyed.

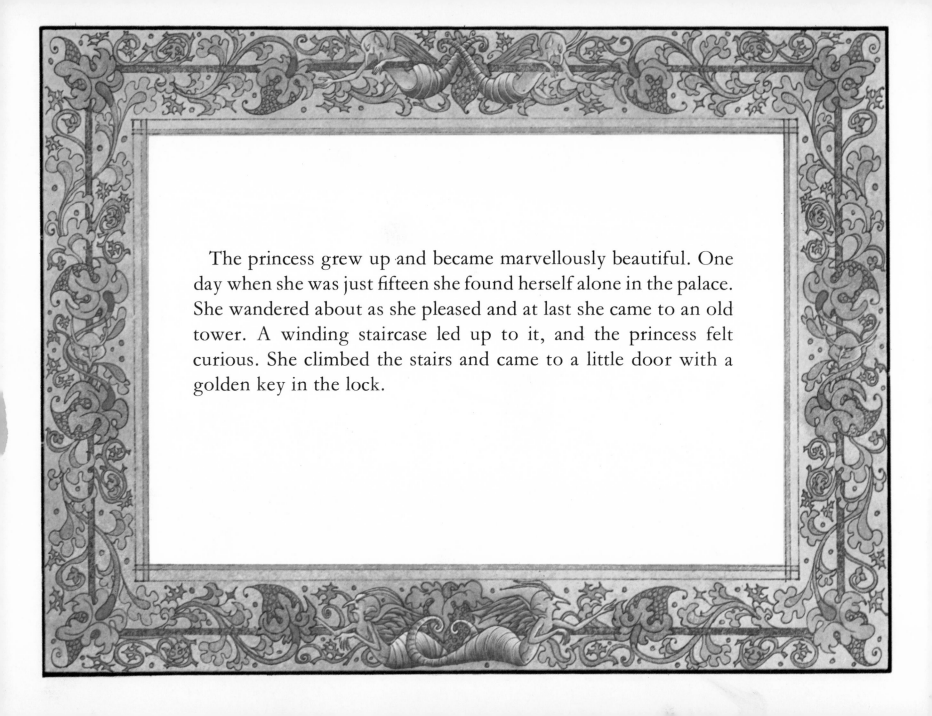

The princess grew up and became marvellously beautiful. One day when she was just fifteen she found herself alone in the palace. She wandered about as she pleased and at last she came to an old tower. A winding staircase led up to it, and the princess felt curious. She climbed the stairs and came to a little door with a golden key in the lock.

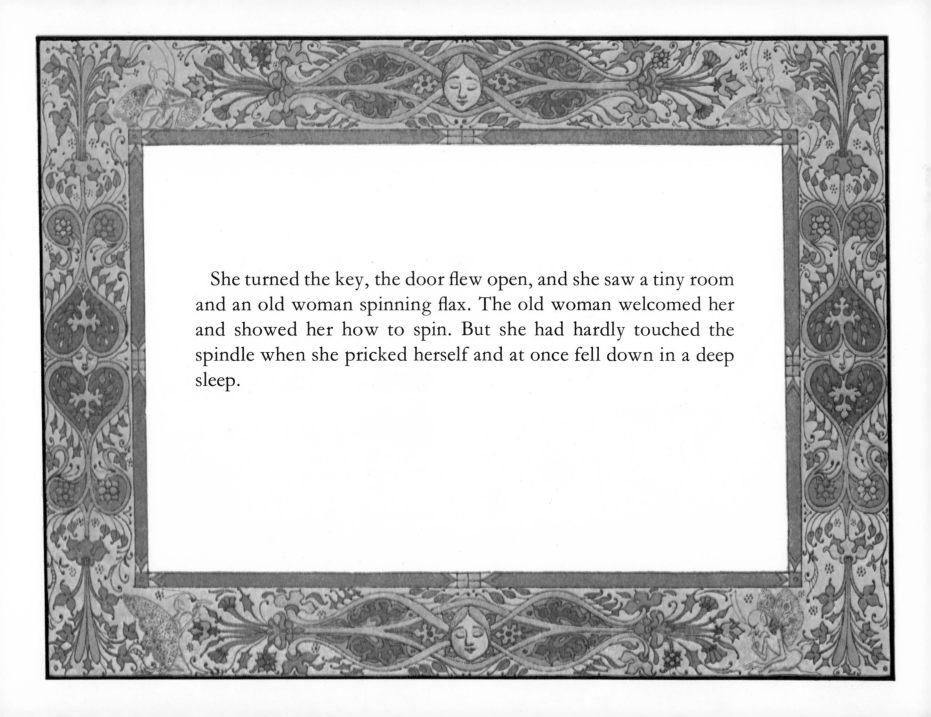

She turned the key, the door flew open, and she saw a tiny room and an old woman spinning flax. The old woman welcomed her and showed her how to spin. But she had hardly touched the spindle when she pricked herself and at once fell down in a deep sleep.

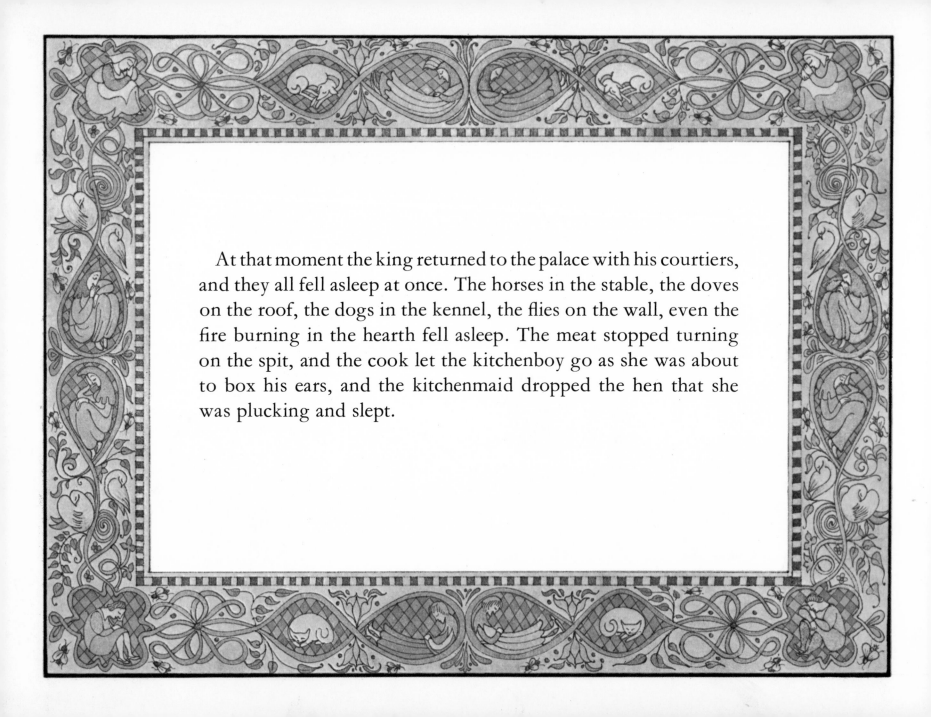

At that moment the king returned to the palace with his courtiers, and they all fell asleep at once. The horses in the stable, the doves on the roof, the dogs in the kennel, the flies on the wall, even the fire burning in the hearth fell asleep. The meat stopped turning on the spit, and the cook let the kitchenboy go as she was about to box his ears, and the kitchenmaid dropped the hen that she was plucking and slept.

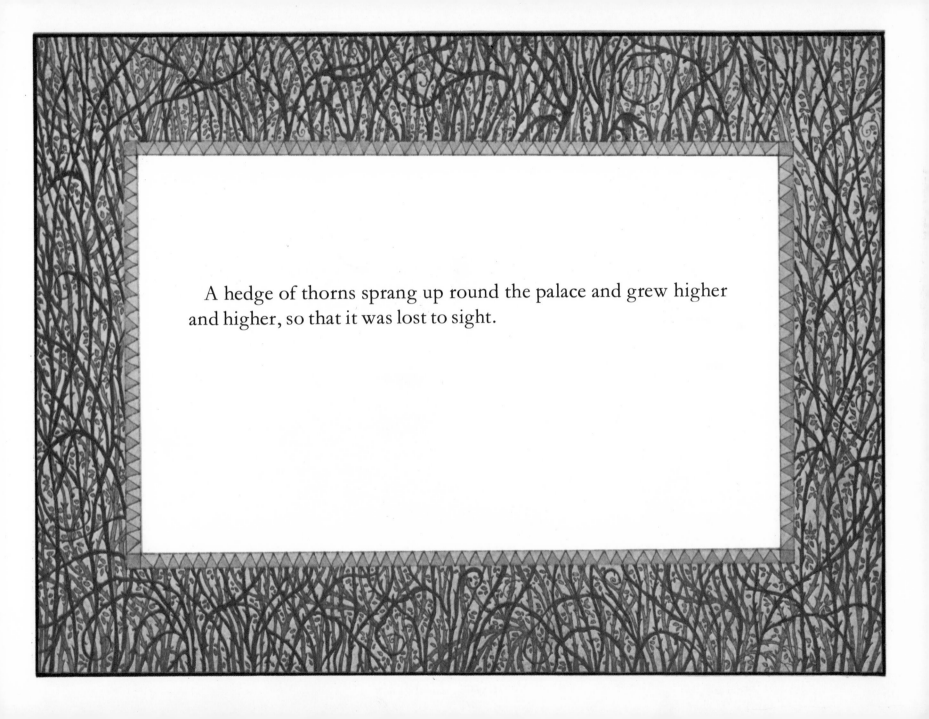

A hedge of thorns sprang up round the palace and grew higher and higher, so that it was lost to sight.

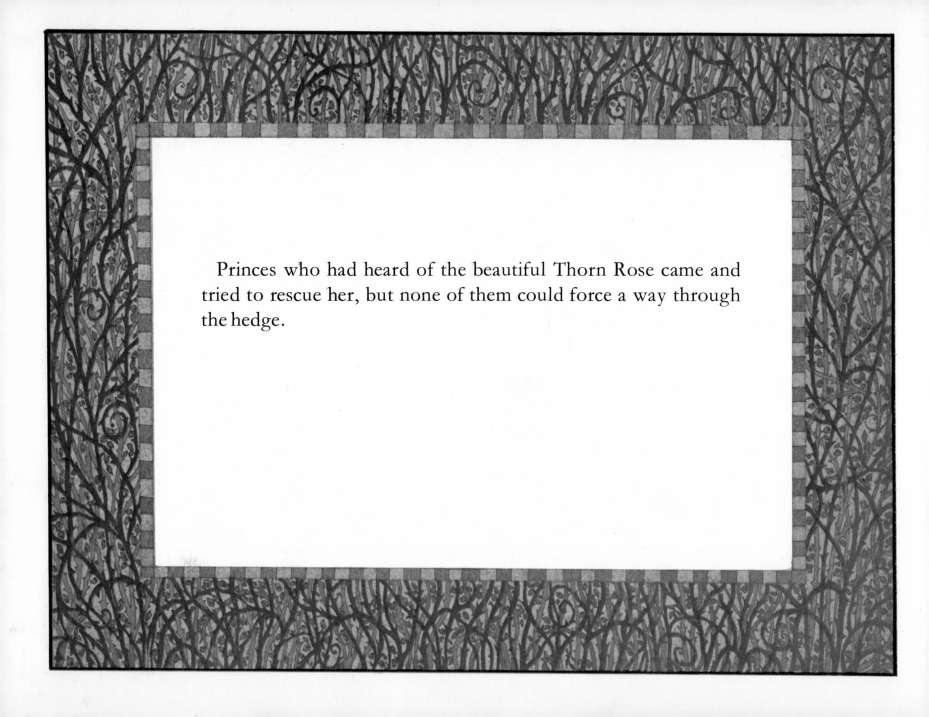

Princes who had heard of the beautiful Thorn Rose came and tried to rescue her, but none of them could force a way through the hedge.

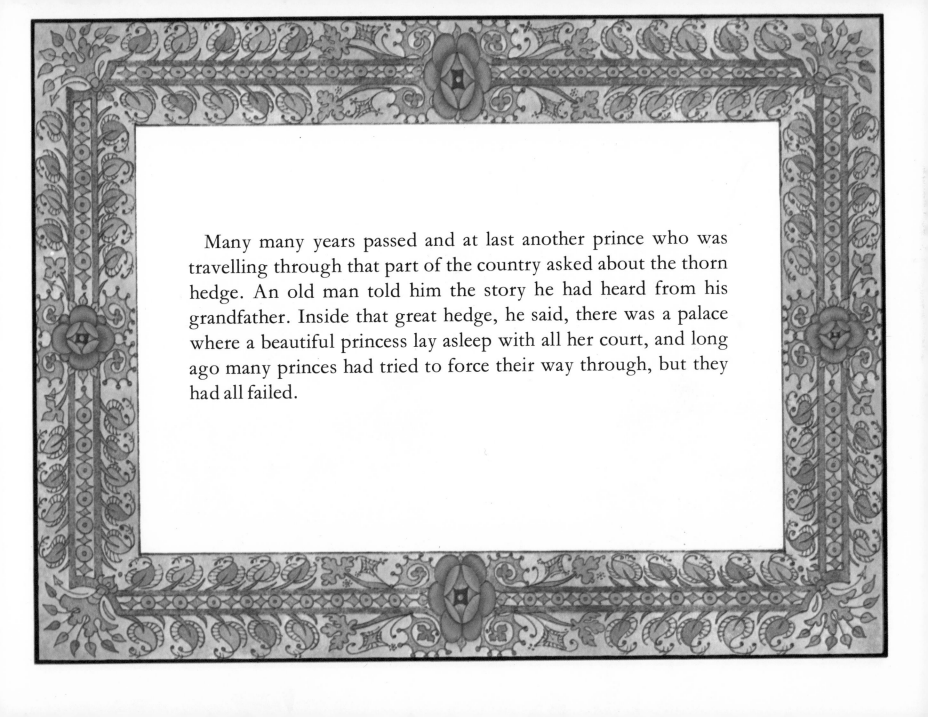

Many many years passed and at last another prince who was travelling through that part of the country asked about the thorn hedge. An old man told him the story he had heard from his grandfather. Inside that great hedge, he said, there was a palace where a beautiful princess lay asleep with all her court, and long ago many princes had tried to force their way through, but they had all failed.

"But I shall succeed," said the prince, "and I shall rescue the lovely Thorn Rose."

As he came up to the hedge, the thorns turned into flowers that parted to let him through, but behind him thorns closed in again. Then he came to a door.

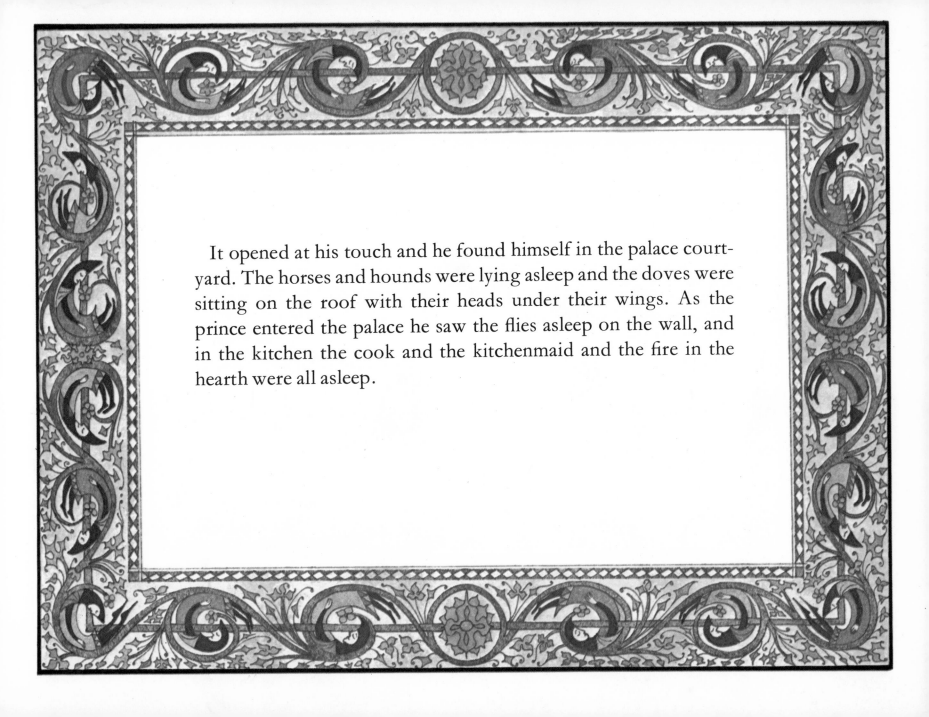

It opened at his touch and he found himself in the palace court-yard. The horses and hounds were lying asleep and the doves were sitting on the roof with their heads under their wings. As the prince entered the palace he saw the flies asleep on the wall, and in the kitchen the cook and the kitchenmaid and the fire in the hearth were all asleep.

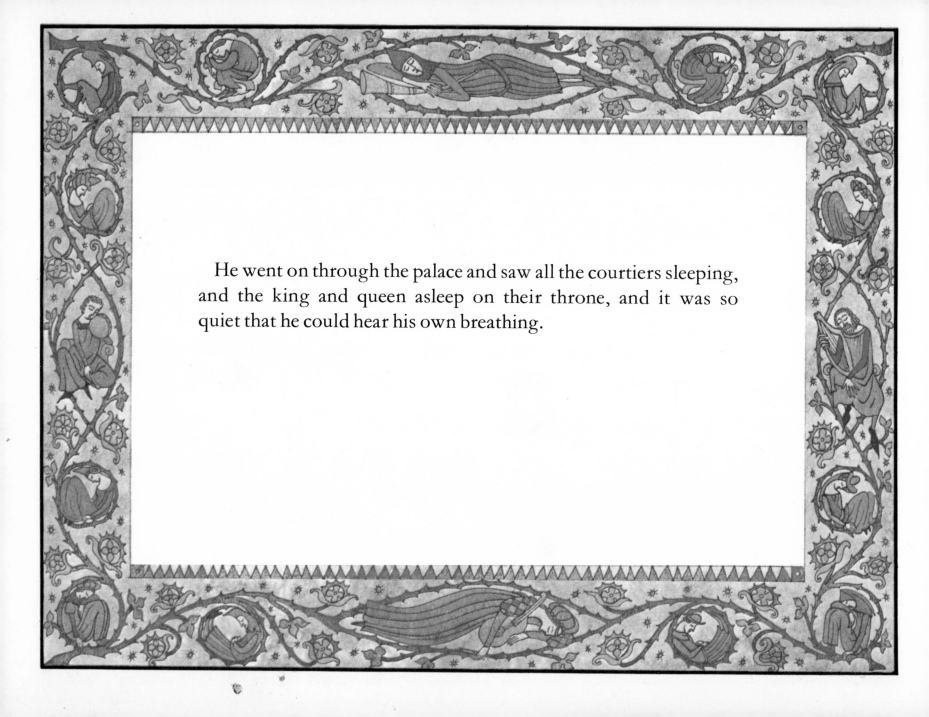

He went on through the palace and saw all the courtiers sleeping, and the king and queen asleep on their throne, and it was so quiet that he could hear his own breathing.

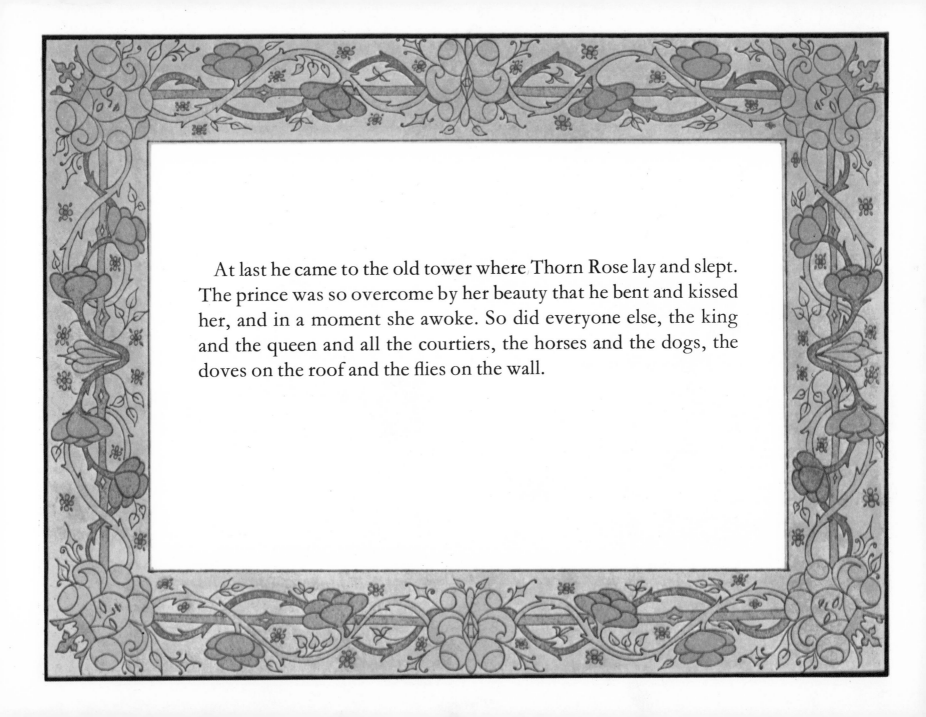

At last he came to the old tower where Thorn Rose lay and slept. The prince was so overcome by her beauty that he bent and kissed her, and in a moment she awoke. So did everyone else, the king and the queen and all the courtiers, the horses and the dogs, the doves on the roof and the flies on the wall.

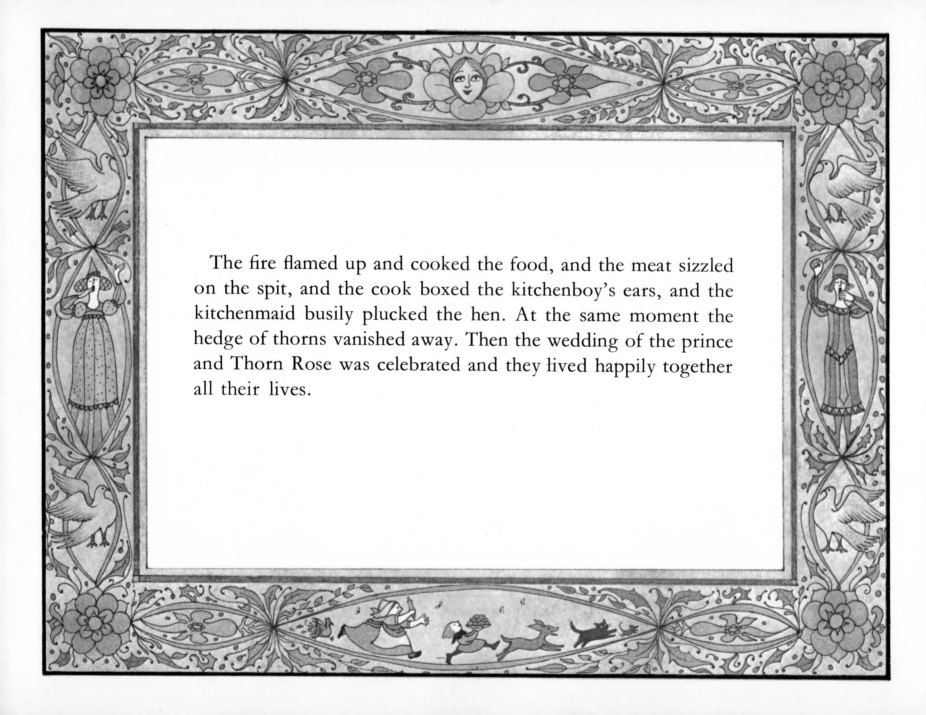

The fire flamed up and cooked the food, and the meat sizzled on the spit, and the cook boxed the kitchenboy's ears, and the kitchenmaid busily plucked the hen. At the same moment the hedge of thorns vanished away. Then the wedding of the prince and Thorn Rose was celebrated and they lived happily together all their lives.